Lee,

Hold onto your
Memories & thanks
for sharing your
birthday with me.

Liz G

2016

Recollections & Reflections

Elizabeth Gentry

Recollections & Reflections
© 2016 Elizabeth Lee "Liz" Gentry

ISBN-13: 978-0-9839485-8-2
ISBN-10: 0-9839485-8-5

Published by TMP Books, 2631 Holly Springs Pkwy. Box 35,
Holly Springs, GA 30142

www.TMPBooks.com

Published in the United States of America.

Only the good times are mentioned here
because the bad experiences are better left unspoken.
Why dig up dirt when it could only hurt someone?

Dedication

I dedicate this to my family, past and present, and to
all my friends that have made me who I am today and
especially to Cheryl Kennedy
who kept encouraging me to tell my story.

Recollections and Reflections

These are memories from my childhood to pass on to family and friends. The stories are true as I remember them. I've tried my best to give an accurate account of growing up in the small town of Dunlap, Tennessee during the 1950s and early 1960s.

People ask me, "Where are you from"? I always reply, "I am a Tennessee Hillbilly, born and raised, dirt poor and couldn't afford dirt."

My story begins with my birth on May 1, 1948 in Dunlap, Tennessee, and I was born and raised in a four room house without indoor plumbing or electricity. Our door latch was just a piece of wood on a nail that we turned to keep the door shut at night and when we were away from the house. No fancy locks or door knobs were ever used. We had a cistern that caught rain water for our use, sometimes having to dip out a frog or two that would be enjoying the cool and dampness. When it ran dry during the summer months we would have to go to the creek and carry up buckets of water to use in cooking and drinking. During the dry months we would carry our laundry down to the creek and have an all-day washday. After all the washing was done, we kids got to play in the creek and float in the washtubs. George would swim into the deep part called the swimming hole and let me hold onto his back, like piggy-back swimming. I couldn't swim and one time he swam out from under me and I sank to the bottom. He had to rescue me and face Mamma about his recklessness. We would stretch lines up between the trees to dry the clothes and we would have lunchmeat sandwiches for lunch.

We didn't get electricity to our house until I was in the fourth grade, after we cleared the right of way for the power lines using axes and cross-cut saws. The wood would be cut into sizes to use as fire wood to keep us warm in the winter. It was a very hard job but we all jumped in and got it done.

Before I get too far into "my story," I believe I should start at the beginning with this family portrait of my grandmother, great-grandmother and great-grandfather and her two brothers. My grandmother was born December 9, 1890. In the next photograph is my grandmother as a young girl along with her parents and her two brothers.

From left to right: Great-Uncle Huston, Great-Grandfather John B Bunch, my Grandmother Sarah Catherine Bunch, Great-Grandmother Cordie and Great-Uncle Marion. I'm not sure how old Mammy was in this picture; I'm guessing about nine or ten. I love her hat.

I don't remember anything about my great-grands. I heard a lot of stories about them. They lived in Rhea County, Tennessee, in the town of Dayton. They were dirt farmers or farm laborers. There is a slight memory of us going across the mountain to visit my Uncle Huston. Can't recall much about it except it was during the hottest part of the summer. Children never got used to just sitting quietly while the adults would get caught up on all of the family news. Of course we did like the food, because we were always asked to stay for dinner or supper. Eating something cooked by someone different than your own family always tastes better when eaten away from home. Guess that is why I like to go out to restaurants on the weekends, the food is always better and I don't have to wash the dishes. It is a win-win situation for everyone.

My grandmother, Sarah Catherine Bunch married John D Farley as they sat in a horse-drawn wagon. She said they just drove up to the preacher's house and he came out to the wagon and performed the marriage ceremony. She even told of couples that were married by "jumping the broom." That was back when she was a very young child.

Papa and Mammy brought their family across the mountain from Dayton, Tennessee, to settle on the Barker Farm in the Sequatchie Valley near the town of Dunlap, Tennessee. A temporary shelter was built to house them that later became known as the smoke house.

This is my grandmother in front of the shelter holding me. She was the greatest influence of my life. She was and still is my hero.

She taught me right from wrong, how to love and respect the simple things in life and to be happy with what we had. I never thought of us as being poor. We were rich even though we had no worldly goods other than a roof over our heads, the clothes on our backs and food on the table; none of the luxuries I have today. One of the most important things she taught me was *"You are only as good as your word*; if you tell someone you will do something, do it; and if you even think that you won't do it, then don't take on the task." The second best thing she taught me was *"never say I can't."* She'd tell me that "*I can't never did do nothing*" and she was right. She told me that I could do anything I wanted to and be anyone I wanted to be if I would just try. You must always try and there is no shame if you are unsuccessful, if at first you tried. At times I would say, Mammy I just can't and she'd say "Did you try?" If I tried that was OK, but if I had not attempted she would make sure I at least gave it my best shot. Sometimes I even succeeded. I still haven't been able to weave a basket, but I have tried many times and failed each time. Just when you think you have the hang of it; it becomes just another woven trivet for pots or bowls.

I have her black clutch bag that she would carry under her arm.

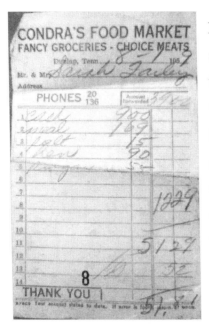

Inside this purse are some tickets from the store where she would do her trading for groceries. Check out the prices and compare them to the prices we pay today for food. Looking back we could buy a 10 pound sack of potatoes for less than $0.50 cents. On some of them you'll see where she charged items that she needed and you will also notice where she had borrowed money to tide her over until the next check day. She was a very honorable woman who could borrow money just upon her word. Everyone knew that she would repay her debts, and she always did. I don't believe I have ever met a more honorable person than Mammy. I still miss her to this day. There is a hole in my heart that will never be filled until I meet her again in Heaven.

Here I am about two years old. The truck I'm in belonged to Z.T. Barker. They probably put me in there to keep me out of their way.

One story that was told of me as a child was that I had a hard time walking bare-footed around the farm. They said I was so tender-footed I would stoop down and brush the small pebbles away, take a step and brush some more away. My folks had to have a lot of patience to put up with me doing that. We were always bare-footed during the summer months, wearing shoes only when we went to church or to town.

Someone photographed me sitting on the ground holding a jonquil. My love of flowers started at a very early age. I'm pretty sure I wasn't supposed to eat them.

I have always called my grandfather, Papa. My only memory of him was running past his sickbed and Papa reaching out his arm and pulling me into his embrace. I can remember feeling his beard against my cheek and hear him say, "No one is going to hurt my baby." Some folks say I can't possibly know this because I had just turned two years old on May 1st and Papa passed away a few days later, on May 8th, his birthday.

My Grandfather, John D Farley. I remember he died on his birthday which always struck me as an odd happening.

I'm not sure of the illness that he had but he was taken care of at home by my grandmother. When she had to do chores such as washing clothes and hanging them on the line to dry, she was always keeping her ears tuned to listen for his ringing of a hand bell to let her know to come to his side. I still have Papa's bell that he would ring when he needed Mammy to come to assist him because he was too sick to get out of bed by himself.

A photograph I titled "Papa's Bell," notice that the handle is hand carved out of a piece of hickory. I have no idea of the age of the bell.

The Barker farm was divided between three siblings, John Bennett Barker, Corrine Johnson and Z.T. Barker. Our home was up on a hill on the section owned by John Bennett and his wife Josephine, everyone called her "Auntie." Everyone that worked on the farm for the Barkers earned 50 cents a day

This is what our churn looked like. We kept it covered with a cloth to keep insects out of it.

each, later I remember that Momma received a $1.00 a day. Momma milked their cow, Peggy, twice a day, the morning milking went to the Barkers and the evening one was ours. She would bring in the bucket of warm milk and we would strain it using a clean flour sack. It sure was good drinking fresh milk. In the hot summer months, we would place our milk in a jug and lower it down into our cistern to keep it cool so it wouldn't spoil. In the winter, we would just leave it sitting on the table in the kitchen because it would be cold enough in the house that it never spoiled. Some mornings we would wake to find ice crystals had formed in the milk. With it being fresh milk, the cream would come to the top and we would skim the butterfat and place it into a gallon Mason jar until we had collected enough to make a churning. My favorite thing to do after school was to churn the cream into buttermilk. While churning, we would sing ... *Come butter come; come butter come, Johnny's at the garden gate waiting on his butter cake, Come butter come.*

Churning took quite a while of slow up and down motion being careful of not hitting the bottom of the churn too hard because you could break it. We then would gather the butter off the top making sure all the liquid was out, add a little salt and put into a special glass bowl that Mammy called the butter mold. It was a life of hard work as farming goes, hoeing corn, planting and gathering crops, herding cattle, but we loved it.

The working helped to provide groceries because

Mamma only drew a Welfare Check of $75.00 a month to feed seven of us. Out of this we paid for food and other necessary items like clothing, shoes, and later power bills. It was slim pickings at our house. One of my memories is all of us walking to town on "check day" to do the grocery shopping. We lived, as the crow flies, about seven or eight miles from town. The closest route was to go across the creek and over the hills and across farms to reach town. If by chance we purchased a lot of supplies, Mr. Condra would drive us home in his pick-up truck, but most time we would all carry our share and walk back home. One Saturday the truck got stuck going up our hill, in a deep rut caused by the rains washing out the roadway. The only time the road got scraped was during election years when the County Commissioner's seat was up for election.

After all the evening chores were completed we would sit out on the porch and listen to a battery powered radio. The stations we would listen to were WSM for the Grand Ole Opry and WCKY-Cincinnati.

Sitting there, talking with family, singing along

with the radio or just listening to the sounds of the night was a wonderful memory. Families don't take the time to talk anymore. Everyone is either watching television, playing on the computer, or the children playing video games, never just talking. I believe if we would do more talking to one another we would have a much happier world.

My Momma, and Aunt Cecil on horses waiting to drive cattle to the mountain pastures; they are bareback. Guess saddles were scarce on the farm. (I can't remember who the young man is.)

My brothers and I would catch lightening bugs and put them in mason jars to use as lanterns. During the summer months, we would catch June bugs and tie a string to one of their legs and fly them like a kite. Guess that wasn't much fun for the bug, but we had a ball watching them fly around. There were many times we would entertain ourselves like this for hours at a time. It was different then, not like today with electronics in hand.

Momma told me of the trips that they would take driving cattle to greener pastures. They would drive the cattle up to their mountain pastures in the spring to graze the grasslands and return them to the valley during the fall to protect them from the snowfalls of the winter months. Momma said these were fun trips, guess it was as close to playing cowboys as you can get.

One task Momma had to do on the farm was to pull fodder for feeding the livestock. They would cut and gather the dried corn stalks into a pile and pull off the dried leaves. This is called fodder. It was good to feed to the cattle during the winter months like folks use baled hay today.

In the next photograph, you will find Momma (in the foreground), my Aunt Paralee, and Z.T. Barker pulling the corn leaves off the stalks. Not a very fun project and it usually lasted several days.

About a half mile up the hill above the Barker's house is where we lived in a four-room house built by lumber culled from the land. You've heard the expression "spitting through the cracks," our house was one where you really could. It was naturally air conditioned during the summer and mighty cold during the winter months, heated by one coal burning stove in the family room and the cook stove in the kitchen.

Posing outside of my bedroom window is Mammy, me and younger brother Johnny.

I remember one of our windows was made up of a type of plastic with threads woven in to strengthen it. It would let in light and it protected us from the elements. My bed that I shared with my grandmother and brother was along this wall.

Living up on a hill like we did, we could watch the storm clouds gather as they came up along the valley. Sometimes we welcomed the rain and other times I dreaded it because of the thunder, lightning and the wind.

Mammy could tell if we were in for bad weather by the way the animals were acting. When frogs are louder than usual bad weather is on its way and when birds are flying high in the sky it is a sign of good weather.

Here you find Mammy looking out the front door checking on me and my brother Johnny. He was a year and a half younger than me. This is one of the photos where I am smiling.

One day it was raining and the wind was blowing just awful and it blew the window down on top of me. It was terrifying trying to get out from under this window. I was yelling and crying and they were trying to get me quieted down as the window fabric was being removed from over me. I suppose it took longer than usual because of me. Seemed like a lifetime back then. I have been scared of storms ever since, still every time it rained I would want to go to sleep. Even today a rainy day is perfect for catching a few zzzs. There is nothing more soothing than to hear rain falling onto a tin roof.

I was a very shy little girl. Every school year visiting teachers came around to all the homes and registered children for school, usually a few weeks before school was to start. I would hear their vehicle coming up the road and I would run out the back door into the woods and stay there until after the strangers would leave. I would also do this whenever anyone would come up the hill to our house. Momma would call me to "Get your-self back here," when it was important that I show up or if it was kinfolk coming for a visit.

The forest was a sanctuary for me. I never grew tired of just sitting on a log or rock listening to the birds and animals scurrying around. I could even hear ants walking on the fallen leaves. I would watch them marching along in line for hours. Sitting alone in the woods reminded me of the Bible where it said to "*Be*

Still, and know that I am God," Psalms 46:10. Every time I had thoughts to work out you could find me alone somewhere just being quiet and still.

Another thing that I would do when I had made Momma mad at me, I would run off into the woods just north of the house and climb up this large oak tree and sit up there and watch her hunt for me. One time I was so scared of getting a whipping that I stayed up there until dark, she shut the door and I had to sit out on the porch until she figured I had been punished enough considering I was scared of the dark. I was a little stinker, yes, that was me alright. I had to say I'm sorry before she would allow me into the house, didn't get spanked but I deserved to.

I went back there after being gone for many years and you know that oak tree just didn't look as big to me then as it did when I was a child. I have been caught up there many times when the cattle would come and hang around in the shade. I wasn't scared of snakes and other critters but those cows really looked big from where I was perched.

It was my chore in the evenings to "slop" the hog. That means I had to carry a bucket of food scraps mixed in with hog feed called Shorts to give to our hog. We used the material that the hog feed came in to make my blouses and dresses.

The area cleared of trees was where we planted and raised our vegetables and across the road was our hog pen where we would fatten out one hog each year; and come November, it was hog killing time.

Here is my Aunt Paralee holding my brother Johnny out at the hog pen.

Someone would kill the hog in November when it was "hog killing weather." That means it was cold. We all would gather to clean and dress it out. One on my chores was scraping the hair off the hide before they strung it up to take out the insides. How we did this was to have boiling water and burlap sacks. The sacks were dipped into the boiling water and laid over the body of the hog. After a few minutes, it was easy to take a dull knife and scrape the hairs away. Another fun but tiring chore was rendering the lard. You would stand over the iron pot and stir with a wooden boat-like paddle until all the lard was cooked out of the fat pieces of meat, resulting into cracklings or now folks call them pig skins. Mammy, that's what everyone called my grandmother, made the best ever crackling cornbread. After the hog had been dressed out and cut up, we had to place it in the salt box that we used to keep the meat from ruining. When we needed some to cook, we would get it out and wash the salt from it and it was good to go; but to this day, I cannot eat salted meat. I have to order the city ham, sugar cured and not salty. Another task was making souse meat. That is when you use all the parts that aren't salted down. It was cooked and placed into clean flour sack tubes that Momma would sew together. My job was to squeeze out all of the grease so that it wouldn't become rancid. We'd then hang it up in the smokehouse until we wanted some to eat. It could be fried or just sliced and put into a biscuit, sort of like Spam. Don't know the last time I ate any; it was a long time ago.

Mammy would always have breakfast for us kids before we left to catch the bus for school. Sometimes it was only a biscuit and Blackstrap Molasses poured over a spoon of butter, other times she would make us Chocolate Gravy. That was a special treat when she did that. Our dinner and supper would consist of just beans and fried taters. We made the most of a pot of pinto beans. The first meal would be beans and cornbread, the next would be the same cooking of pintos but since there would be much less beans she would make dumplings and drop them into the bean soup. Bean dumplings are very good, if you've never had them give it a try, I believe you will love them like we did. Every once in a while we would have a pinto bean pie for dessert. No matter what was put before us to eat, we ate it because a favorite saying of my grandmother was *"Eat and play shut mouth."* You never complained about the food, if you did you just didn't get to eat. She would sometimes tell us to clean our plates because there were starving kids in Africa that would appreciate food like we had. Never figured out how she knew this but we ate what was put before us and didn't complain. There was no fooling around at the table, it was a place to eat, not play around. Everyone ate at the same time and sitting around the table was a fun and blessed time.

Foods that we foraged …

Sometimes food was scarce and Momma would go down along the creek banks and pick water cress. She loved "cresses" as she called them. We ate a lot of wild greens. My favorite was wild lettuce and green onions with hot bacon grease poured over it along with some cornbread. Yummy and then I would take a nap because for some reason, it always relaxed me and made me sleepy. Using the leafy lettuce from the grocery store is similar but just not the same. Mammy would also go out and pick a basket of assorted greens. I call them weeds these days. She would clean and wash them and boil them like we do turnip greens. I would probably poison myself if I tried it today. In the spring, we would take four bed sheets and head off down the hill toward the banks of the Sequatchie River to gather Sarvisberries to make jam and jelly out of. Sarvisberry, sometimes called serviceberry, is a small tree or large shrub that grows a sweet round fruit. We would spread the sheets out under the tree and shake the tree to get the berries to fall off. It was fun and we would always sneak a handful ever once in a while; guess we ate about as many as we picked up. Another treat I remember eating is the fruit from the Mulberry tree. It had a long type of fruit and me and the birds loved it. It is amazing that I didn't poison myself. Something else that we picked a lot of back then was wild plums. They grew on shrubs and were plentiful especially along roadsides and branches. They made good eating as we picked them for use in making jellies. You can't find them anymore, don't know why they disappeared. Picking blackberries was a lot of fun too, except for the chiggers and the wasps. I found a bush once that had the biggest blackberries I had ever seen. When I started picking them, I heard a buzzing sound and realized I was about to be covered with some really big red wasps. Down went the bucket and off I ran. Had to wait until they calmed back down to retrieve my bucket and look for another bush to pick from. Oh and then there is Poke Sallet (Pokeweed). When it first begins to grow in the spring and is very tender, Mamma would pick it, wash it several times and parboil it, drain off the water several times during the boiling process because the roots are poisonous, then she would place it in the frying pan to finish cooking it. She would sometimes add scrambled eggs to it. I never acquired a taste for it but the family loved it. She said when I was two days old she gave me a taste of the juices from it, maybe that's why I'm like I am today. Now when the Poke stalks were still tender, we would cut them up like okra, bread them and fry them. It was good eating back then before the okra from our garden was ready to pick.

We had a cellar dug out under the kitchen where we stored Irish and sweet potatoes and all of our canned goods for the winter. To keep insects out of the potatoes we dusted them with lime. It seemed to do the trick.

Canning our vegetables was an ongoing chore during the summers. Mammy tried her best to teach me how to do this but I wasn't very interested in learning. My job was to wash the jars because my hands was small enough to reach the bottom and the they had to be very clean and sterilized in boiling water before they were filled. This could go on for days. The jars of green beans, peaches, apples, pickled beets, sauerkraut, and cucumber pickles would be safe from spoiling in the summer and from freezing in the winter. We would place straw over them during the winter to protect them. It had a musty smell down there in the dark.

Another way we preserved our food was the drying method. Onions were pulled with their blades still attached and we would tie them into bundles and hang them up until they were needed. We made leather britches by stringing green beans on heavy thread and hanging them up to dry. When they were dried out they would last until we were ready for them to be cooked. Apples were sliced and laid onto sheets up on the roof to dry. This was a way to have apple pies and cobblers during the winter months.

We would sometimes go down to the lower bottom toward the river around a little pond and gather small branches from the Spicewood shrub. These would be broken into short pieces and boiled to make Spicewood tea. It was real good when sweetened. We also gathered Sassafras roots to make tea.

Meats that we ate were squirrel and rabbit, these made great dumplings. There was deer, coon, an occasional goat and even muskrat. I always tell people, "*You will eat anything when you are hungry.*" Yes, I can remember being hungry. I have at times left the house at suppertime and took with me a biscuit and find wild onions to eat, so that my younger brothers would have more from our table.

There were always biscuits or cornbread cooked and on the shelf above the stove for a quick munching when the urge hit us. My favorite was when the cornbread stuck to the skillet, Mammy would leave it and it would curl up as it continued to cook as the skillet cooled down. It would be very crispy and very tasty. Today, you can get a similar treat in a bag of Sun-chips. I learned to make cornbread when I had to stand in a chair to reach the table to mix it up. Mammy made sure I could do it right and today I still bake a mighty good pone of cornbread. Cornbread and milk was our supper meal many times. When we had fresh churned buttermilk, it would be buttermilk and cornbread. I also remember Mamma cooking "mush," that's boiled cornmeal. Like I said it was slim pickings at our house at times. Another treat we would have is 'parched' corn. You take whole kernel corn shelled off the cob and place it into hot grease and cook it until it was parched. You had to have good teeth to chew it. It is similar to the kernels that don't pop when you pop popcorn.

Sarah Catherine Farley, known to all who knew her as Mam or Mammy.

I was asked many times to 'look' the dried beans that Mammy wanted to cook. There I would find small stones and sometimes sticks from the bean packing plant. After looking the beans she would wash them and place them into a pot to soak overnight. The next day we would feast on beans and cornbread.

Another of my fondest memories was coming home from school and find Mammy in the kitchen with an iron pot on the stove as she cooked our supper. After giving her a hug and telling her I had missed her while I was at school, I would lift up the cover and gaze upon a pot of butter beans (the large white Lima Beans) and being the little stinker that I was, would say "Yum, Yum, Maggot Stew," and Mammy would very quickly pop me in the mouth and say "Sister, you know better than that." It became a game just between the two of us. To this day I still enjoy eating butter beans just as a tribute to the greatest lady that has ever lived.

I recall the first time that I realized she was getting old. I had been up to no good and she had a hickory in her hand to give me a whipping and I ran from her. She came after me and I would crawl up the bank and under the barbed wire fence and she would follow, then down under the fence and back into the road. This went on back and forth for a while until I looked back and she was heading back to the house. I thought I had gotten away scot free. What I didn't realize was that she hadn't forgotten whatever it was that I had done and was waiting on me when I returned home; and as I stepped inside, this hand clamped down upon my arm and did I ever get a whipping. I never ran from her again. The lesson I learned from it was *"if you do something wrong at least stand and take your punishment."*

Johnny and me, I love this red dotted-Swiss dress. It was one of only 5 brand new dresses I can ever remember having.

"*I Don't Know*" didn't live at our house like he lives in many homes. When we were asked "Who done this?" it was expected that the guilty person would own up to it and say "I did it." Punishment was easier if you told the truth.

I probably got a whipping every day and twice on Sunday, and deserved most of them. I quickly learned that the big switches didn't hurt quite as much as the smaller ones. Momma would get my brother Johnny to get a switch for my punishment and I would have to get one for his punishment. Bet you know where this is going... I would beg Johnny please don't get a big one and he would, thinking he would pull one over on me and bring a switch about the size of his little finger. Momma would give me my dose of "Hickory Tea" and when I had to get one for Johnny, yes, I would gather a very skinny, limber one that would almost bring blood, sometimes it did. Brothers and sisters always tried to outdo the other, but he never caught on that he was getting the worse part of it all. I wonder now if that is why you hardly ever see me smiling in my photos. Maybe I was feeling a little guilty of being such a stinker.

I call this my pin-up pose.
Don't you just love my expression?

Many little girls would have Paper-Dolls to play with but I never did. I would cut out pictures from the Sears catalog and find clothes to fit the model and that was my paper-dollies. I used to wish for some real Paper-Dolls for Christmas or my birthday but that was just a waste of money that we didn't have.

Come Christmastime, we would go out and cut a tree and bring it in to trim. Most of our trimmings were handmade. Some were crocheted and others were sticks that we covered with colorful papers or pictures cut from the Sears and Roebuck Catalog. That was one good use from that catalog, the other was it usually stayed out in our outhouse as the only toilet tissue we had. Ours was a one seater. I just don't see why there would be more than one in there. I've seen pictures of two-seaters, but honest, would you want to share space as you did your business? Not me.

In the background, you can see our "little brown shack" where we did our business. George, my older brother is rinsing his hair using a teakettle of warm water as our dog, Ole Possum, looks on.

I remember having to relocate our outhouse once, due to the pit filling up. We just moved away from it and dug another pit. While one would dig, one would be on top with a bucket tied to a rope to pull out the dirt when it got too deep to just throw the dirt out with a shovel. One time I was in the pit and George, he is seven years older than me, pulled the ladder out and left me until Mammy made him get me out.

It was pranks like that which kept us together as a family. We had to have fun some way to make the chores more enjoyable. I still believe that if you can't have fun doing your job, you should just stay in bed. I have put this philosophy to work all of my life. There have been times that I didn't want to get up, but when I'm up I wanted to be at work, especially when I landed the job as the research librarian at the Booth Western Art Museum. I'll come back to this later, because that would be skipping too much of my past to leave it here.

Another short confession, I'm scared of the dark. I could hear all of the evil critters moving around in the dark and my imagination would run wild. You just never caught me outside after sundown unless it was totally necessary. Even now as an adult, I don't like to be outside when darkness falls.

When I had to go do my business before bedtime, I would carry my little brother Billy with me. He was my security blanket.

Here you will find my Aunt Paralee holding my youngest brother Billy and Mammy holding my brother Junior.

Mammy asked me one time, "Sister, why do you

carry your baby brother with you when you attend to your business?" I very seriously answered her with, "If anything gets after me I will sit Billy down and run." I know, not very nice of me but I probably would have just thrown him to the wolves, if there had been wolves. Billy was injured in a car accident when he was three months old and had seizures until his death at the age of five and a half years old. He was the sweetest young man. When he was about two years of age he could let us know when a seizure was coming on by motioning to us with his hand as if to say come here. He died of a brain aneurysm. He is still missed dearly. I often wonder what kind of young man he would have become.

When I was about eight years old, around the second grade, it was finally time for me to take to the corn fields to hoe the corn like everyone else. George was to show me how it was done. He took me to the field, showed me the rows that I was to hoe and went on to do his own hoeing. Well, he didn't explain that young corn and Johnson's Grass looked the same when they are about 3 or 4 inches high. I proceeded to destroy 2 rows of corn before he came to check on me. Needless to say that was the end of my field work. I was taken home and was assigned to ZT and Lucille's house to do inside work. ZT ran a dairy and sold eggs from his chicken houses. He had me washing and grading eggs out in one end of the milking barn. He sold the eggs by the crateful. When I finished up there, I would mop and hand wax their hardwood floors. Wax on, wax off. It was an all day job down on my knees, just like Cinderella. They were a great influence on me as I grew up, taking me to Bible School during the summer and they took me to see my first movie. It was "*This is Cinerama*", the first motion picture that put you in the picture. It was amazing. This is how I told Momma when I got home. "*It was amazing, Momma, we flew over and down into the Grand Canyon in Arizona, over the glaciers in Alaska, and rode the world's highest rollercoaster.*" Well Momma really burst my bubble when she said "*if you're going to come home lying like that you will just stay home the next time they want to take you anywhere.*"

I can hear her now. She just didn't understand

but that's what we did...

Lucille had bought me a new black skirt and a white blouse, like the one worn by Dr. Ben Casey on TV. I was so proud of the new outfit. It was one of only 6 new outfits/dresses I remember ever having. All of my clothes were bought at the Rag Store in town or we made them out of feed-sack material or from clothes that we took apart and recycled. Mamma had a foot pedal Singer sewing machine. I learned to sew by watching her. She could make beautiful things with so little to work with.

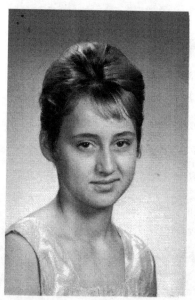

This is a blouse that I made, it was simple, made from feed-sack material, but I loved wearing it. I was in the ninth grade when this photo was taken at Sequatchie County High School.

I began sewing during the second grade at about eight years of age. I loved sewing and making new things. We had a peddle Singer Sewing Machine, as a small child I would sit on the pedal and ride while momma sewed. One Christmas I made aprons for all the womenfolk on the farms, using scraps of cloth that you could buy by the bag full from the shirt factory in town. I was one proud little girl as I went around to their homes to deliver their presents. They seemed to love them.

I learned to crochet by sitting at my Mammy's knees as she crocheted. Her fingers would go so fast it was like watching a machine. It was many years later while crocheting with a friend that I realized that by learning by watching and repeating the moves that she was doing, that I was crocheting backward or wrong side out. My work was a mirror image of how it was supposed to be done. Baby blankets, baby sweaters and booties and matching caps, ponchos and afghans are just o few of the items that I crocheted. I have to admit that when making stuffed animals, my way was much more attractive than the regular way it was supposed to be done. The texture was different and the patterns more pronounced. Of course, many folks said then and even now that I'm sort of backwards.

Before we got electricity up to our house we would all walk down to John and Auntie's on Thursday night to watch their television. What a treat, we would watch The Adventures of Rin Tin Tin, the story of a German shepherd dog and his companion Rusty who had been rescued from an Indian attack on their wagon train. They lived at Fort Apache in Arizona and were the sidekicks for "B" Company with Lieutenant Rip Masters and the soldiers that help to bring law and order to the early west. They had many adventures together and when Rusty needed Rin-Tin-Tin to do something special or to save someone he would yell "Yoooooo Rinty."

It's amazing to think back at your earliest heroes. After that we would watch Dragnet featuring Sergeant Joe Friday starring Jack Webb. This was a detective mystery. The only bad thing about this was walking back up the hill in the dark, remember, I was very scared of the dark. I could imagine all kinds of evils hiding alongside of the dirt road especially after watching episodes of The Mummy and Dracula. The Mummy was my most terrifying shows that I watched back then. I could hear it coming after me in the dark, the dragging of his foot as he reached out his hand as if to grab me and carry me away with

him. My imagination ran wild, very wild.

The dark still holds a terror that I can't release. I don't watch horror films now, even turn my head away or shut my eyes when there is an advertisement on television. The images will linger with me for days should I see any scary movies. Just give me a good or even a not so good western love story or a Longmire mystery and I'm a happy camper. I will get lost among the lines and block out everything around me, much to my husband's aggravation.

It was a treat when George bought our first television when he worked at the factory after school. It was a small black and white and we could only get three channels, 3, 9 and 12 out of Chattanooga.

George was my first and only sibling to graduate from high school. He attended the Sequatchie County High School. Here he is receiving his diploma.

Another confession, this is a really silly one, but remember now how I was raised, I actually thought the people on TV could see me in our living room. When it was time to bathe before going to bed, I would line up chairs and using quilts for privacy as I sponged off each night. I'll pause here so that you can gather yourself from laughing so hard … I later learned that I was safe and that no one could watch me bathe. I was also fascinated with the light that came on when I opened the refrigerator. When they coined the phrase "You've come a long way baby" I surely have. Looking back I wonder how I could have been so naïve. Living back in the country as I did, it took a lot of learning to grasp the way others lived their lives. Of course, I never felt like I was poor, we had all we needed and we were loved.

Once while I was supposed to be cooking supper, frying potatoes to be exact, I heard Bobby Rydel as he was announced on American Bandstand by Dick Clark. This show was all the rage with the teens back then. I turned away from the stove to watch as he performed and did not notice the glow of flames from the kitchen stove. The grease that I was to fry the potatoes in had caught fire and was blazing up toward the ceiling. The ceiling had caught fire, but we noticed it in time, that Momma was able to put out the fire to save the house.

I grabbed the skillet and threw it out of the door that was right by the stove, never thinking to put a lid over the flames and the hot grease splashed back onto my right arm. The lucky part about this whole episode was, I had on a sleeveless blouse and only my arm was burned. I received second and third degree burns from my pointer finger up to my elbow. At first I was so scared that I didn't realize that I was burnt, I ran outside while Mamma put out the fire and saved our home. When the pain finally reached my shocked mind, I came in and Mammy took out our camphorated salve and lathered my whole arm. The blisters were already forming and she immediately wrapped it up in clean flour sack bandages. This all took place just before the 4th of July and I had to go to town with my arm wrapped up in white flour sack material to keep the blisters protected. Everyone that saw me asked did I break my arm and I had to explain. I have only two small scars to remind me to never leave grease or oil on a hot stove.

It was around this time that the Barker's got together and decided that my Momma shouldn't be doing farm labor such as hauling hay and the heavy work, so she went to town and found a job at the local shirt-factory. She was good at sewing. I remember her coming home and saying that she had to sign her name on her time card and that she didn't know how to write or to spell her name. I told her that I would help her learn how to do that. We worked many hours on the weekend and finally she was able to sign in cursive, Josie Farley. She was so proud of herself because now she wouldn't have to just make her X on papers and at the bank she could cash her payroll check.

Our house was up on a ridge across a holler where the main road was that led into the farms. We could hear vehicles coming along that road and that really came in handy on mornings that we were late getting ready for school. We'd hear the bus coming and Mammy would say "Ya'll hurry up now and don't you miss that bus." We would take off running downhill to the Johnson's and would get there just as the bus was turning around. When we were early Miss Corrine would let us come in and watch television while we waited. The Today Show with Dave Garraway would be on and I remember he had this chimp on there with him sometimes. His name was J. Fred Muggs and he was dressed up in people clothes and sometimes would act up and throw a tantrum. It was a fun show to watch back then. When we would have to catch the bus and it was raining I had a long heavy wool coat that I'd wear and then leave it on the back porch to dry and pick it up in the evening. We didn't have rain gear back then.

My favorite bus driver was a man by the name of Avery Deakins. He was a very caring man. Since we were the first on the bus in the morning and the last off in the afternoon, he got to know his riders quite well. Most mornings he would give me a sausage biscuit for my breakfast. He'd say "The missus made some extra this morning and we don't want them to go to waste."

Our bus route took almost two and a half hours to complete the run from pickup to delivery at Dunlap Elementary School. One year we rode the early bus and the next year our route was the second bus trip. On the late years we would get to wait in the auditorium and watch television until it was time to board. This was where I took a liking to the World Series. I remember watching the New York Yankees play and I admired Whitey Ford, who was a great pitcher and Roger Maris one of the best outfielders who hit 61 home runs in 1961. I still like watching the Series each year, not the games building up to it, just the championship games.

George was very popular at school. He was very smart and he played sports. His football outfits as I remember was so hard to get clean. We made our own lye soap and used that for bathing, washing dishes and for washing clothes. Using a rubboard to get the grass stains out was not an easy task. He was a neat freak as we would say these days as you can see in the next two photographs.

Here are two photos of George, look at those creases in his pants. They were put there by me using an iron that you set on the stove to warm up.

When hanging his pants on the line to dry I would insert these metal things called stretchers, they helped with putting creases into the pant legs.

When he started dating, he would change into clean clothes two or three times on Saturday. He said he couldn't wear the same clothes with different girls. He was a playboy back then. He even told of how he would come up behind a cute girl driving down the road and tap her rear bumper so that she would stop and they could exchange phone numbers. Today he would probably get arrested for a stunt like that.

One of my favorite memories while waiting on the school-bus was when George would comb my hair. I would run a brush over it and leave the tangles hidden beneath, but he would always find them. I never had to go to school with tangled up hair. He said I let the rats sleep in comfort for they always made a good rat-bed. Big brothers can sometimes be really nice.

And Speaking of Ratty Hair...

My sister Mary Jane is holding me along with her husband Silas Pursley. I hope they finally combed my hair.

Two weeks before I started to school, I had to go and stay in town with my sister, Mary Jane. She is 14 years older than I am. She had married Silas Pursley and moved to town a few years before. She was the one who took me to get all of my shots that were required to enter the first grade and to get me registered. She also would take me some Saturdays on the bus across the mountain to Chattanooga to do her shopping. We mostly looked in the stores and ate at a cafeteria and then back to Dunlap in the evening. Those were fun times that I got to share with her and the memories I still hold dear.

On one return trip on the bus she noticed that I was a little flushed and had a slight fever, well, I was coming down with the measles. It turned out to be the three day measles and to this day I still have not had the two week measles. Guess I am lucky for that. The old family doctor said that I must be immune to them because I was always around brothers and cousins who had them. I can't remember having any childhood diseases except the mumps and then they were only on one side. Don't ask me why, I don't understand it either. I do know that if I am ever around someone who has the mumps my left jaw will hurt. Maybe it's all in my head. Something has to be in there…Giggle, Giggle.

Let's talk a little about our country Christmas at

our house…

We didn't get very many toys like kids do now, we were lucky to get just one and maybe some clothes. In this next photograph, you see I received a doll and Johnny received a new set of clothes.

I know I'm not looking too happy but it is because I'm being made to stand still against the house for a Christmas photograph. There is that same ratty hair-do. I did get better somewhat by getting my hair manageable.

When I was 10 years old I found out that my
brother Johnny was getting a bicycle for Christmas

and instead of being happy for him, I became a selfish
little brat. Here is a picture of George riding the bike
that was just a little too big for Johnny at the time but
he did finally grow into it.

I threw a fit and told
Mamma that if I didn't
get a record player I just
didn't want anything that
"Santa" would bring me.
Realize now that we
didn't have much money
to buy anything extra
with. We were lucky to

get food and needed clothing, but here I was being very hateful. Well I'm not sure what she had to do to get it but this is what was under the tree with my name on the tag.

There were three 75 rpm records with it, and the only song that I remember is...

"Don't be scared of thunder, it's nothing but a great big sound. Don't be scared of lightning, it hardly ever hit's the ground. Just be very careful and you'll be safe as can be. Take shelter in a house or barn but never underneath a tree."

When we as children ask for or as in this instance, demand something we never see the sacrifices that our parents and loved ones go through to make us happy. That player probably cost at the most $5.00, but that would be a whole week of hard work for Mamma at that time. Johnny got his bicycle and along with our usual apple, orange, stick-candy and some nuts, we were happy.

Thinking back, it would have been a great Christmas with just the fruit and candy. I never again was that selfish at Christmas. It is hard even now to ask for something, even when others ask "What do you want for Christmas this year?" I suppose everyone should be thankful for the little things we have and not be wishing for something that is out of our reach.

On a more, happier memory around Christmas time was Momma making her fruit cakes. She would begin gathering supplies months before and storing them to keep us kids from getting into them. Back then you would buy raisins in round cakes. She would buy the dark raisins and the lighter raisins. Bags of mixed nuts and walnuts were hidden away and we would all pitch in when it came to cracking the nuts, preparing them for her cakes. Wish I had her recipe but it is lost and those wonderful cakes will be no more.

There would also be wonderful Teacakes that Mammy would make. Why didn't I get that recipe? They were the most delicious cookies that I've ever eaten.

When I was nine years old Mama baked me this

birthday cake. She even bought the hard candy icing decorator candies to go on it, along with nine candles. I can't recollect ever having a real "birthday party" just a homemade cake for a Sunday dinner. I would have to go out and chase down the chicken so that we would have either fried chicken or chicken dumplings. Our Sunday dinners were always the highlight of the week, with food enough that we all had a full tummy when all was gone. Of course by this time in my life it was up to me to wash the dishes after such a celebration, birthday or not.

I loved attending school. It got me away from the isolation of the house on the hill. I went to Dunlap Elementary School's first through eighth grades.

My teachers made a big impression upon me to always do my best. My grades were pretty good, mostly A and Bs. My teachers were Miss Grace Hudson, 1st grade, Miss Anna Lee Harmon, 2nd grade, Miss Lorene Seals (my favorite), 3rd. grade, Miss Ilene Richards, 4th grade, Miss Pauline Hale, 5th grade, Miss Letha Pratt, 6th, Miss Patsy Pope, 7th grade, and Mr. Ray Maby, 8th grade. The Principle was Mr. Overton Johnson. Every other week Miss Viva Rogers would come and teach Art and Miss Nannie Bell Clark taught us the Bible. These were all great folks who were dedicated to teaching and raising us children to be the best students that we could be.

Each morning we would stand and say the Pledge of Allegiance to the American Flag, then there were announcements over the intercom and then we would begin classwork.

First Grade

In the first grade Miss Hudson would always have the class lay our heads down on our table after lunch to rest. We were supposed to be quiet and still. Once she caught me rolling my pencil across the table to a girl on the other side and I was taken out into the hall and paddled. No more pencil rolling after that.

Second Grade

In the second grade, Mrs. Holland always wore high heels and we could hear as she came down the hall to our classroom. We were supposed to stay in our seats whenever she left the room but did we? No! She finally figured it out and came in holding her shoes and we all had to give up our recess period for the rest of the week. We kind of learned a lesson there also.

Third Grade

In the third grade, Miss Seals was my favorite teacher. She allowed me to have extended sleep sessions after lunch. I always completed my work in a timely manner and she rewarded me this way, sleeping through the third grade.

Fourth Grade

In the fourth grade, I learned that I was handicapped by having a family that couldn't help me with my reading. Except for George, he did his best to see that I read my assignments as I should. Mrs. Richards would have each of us to stand up by our desks and read a paragraph or page from our Social Studies book. I was reading about Hippocrates and since I read it phonetically so I read it as Hip-o-crates, the whole class laughed at me, which added to my shyness. I refused to read aloud after that.

My fifth and sixth grades went by uneventful; I enjoyed learning and was becoming a much better student.

The seventh grade got me another spanking for standing up to Mrs. Pope because of her mistreating my friend Phyllis, or at least I thought she was. Out in the hall we went and she took her paddle along with her.

The eighth grade was fun. Learning more and more and was allowed to walk up to the high school, which was in yelling distance to catch the bus home in the evenings. Well I found out where the fuse box was and would loosen the fuses so that when the janitor came in the next day he would have to tighten them up before the lights would come back on. I know now that I shouldn't have done that but it was fun especially since I didn't get caught. The lesson here is NOT to do things that cause others more work even if you aren't harming anyone or anything.

Ninth Grade

High school was a lot harder than the eighth grade, but there were boys, the cause of my downfall. My mind was not always on schoolwork as most children that age were in the same boat.

My favorite subject was Geography, taking me too many foreign lands, anything to get me away from the hill I lived upon. My least favorite was Math, still have trouble with numbers. While in high-school I took algebra for a year and ½ and never completed an equation. Mrs. Grace Patton gave us credit for each step we completed. It was the only thing that saved me from failing.

Speaking of high-school, I dropped out after the first half of my sophomore year, got married and moved to South Georgia. Sounded exciting to a 15 year old at the time, but lessons were learned by the school of hard knocks. Life was good and bad but I survived. I gave birth to two wonderful children, a son, Barney Joe Turner and a daughter, Marchelle Renee Turner.

They have each given me two beautiful grandchildren that I've enjoyed watching grow up and make a living of their own.

 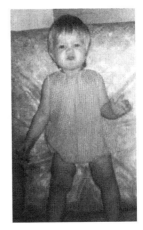

My advice to anyone who is thinking about quitting school, DON'T! You will live to regret it, stay in school and get your education; it is definitely easier to learn when you are young. I did eventually get my GED and also went to college to learn a trade. It was a struggle but it helped me land a wonderful job that later lead me to become the librarian/archivist at the Booth Western Art Museum, a dream job that I love. I had to learn by the self-taught way and it wasn't easy but I never gave up.

Now for another memory that just came floating by…

One Sunday in May would be Decoration Day at Chapel Hill Cemetery. It would be an all-day event, with dinner on the ground and singing after lunch. Folks would come from miles around, a great homecoming for everyone. Mamma and Mammy would fry chicken, cook green beans and cornbread and we would take wild flowers or flowers made from crepe paper to decorate Papa's and our other relatives that had gone on before us. This is where most all of my relatives are buried. Kids would play tag and other fun games that kids play. The elders would sit and catch up on all of the local news and gossip. We would see some that we hadn't seen in years. Now I will tell you the truth, it was hard on us young'uns to stay well behaved all day in front of so many strangers, but somehow we managed. Below is a photograph of me and my two little brothers in front of Papa's stone.

This was taken in May of 1958, I was 10 years old, Johnny was 8 and Junior was just a tiny baby.

As you can see I was trying to smile and look like I really wanted to be there, especially since I loved having my photo taken. That evening we would walk all over the cemetery looking at all of the pretty flowers. The well-to-do folks would place real, store bought arrangements and they would smell so good, but most of ours were homemade arrangements placed there with love and affection.

Let me tell you about another episode in my life on the hill. It was a windy spring day and I was very bored. It was our routine every spring to burn off the garden spot to get it ready for planting. Momma was in the house getting her hair cut and permed and couldn't come outside to watch the fire. She told me multiple times Not to set a fire because it was just too windy. Did I listen? You guessed right, I didn't. I went out there and dropped a match into the very dry grass and weeds that had taken over the garden spot. You know the rest, it flared up and before I knew it, it had reached the pasture and was headed for the woods. I screamed for help and Momma had just gotten to the spot where she could wrap a towel around her hair and she and Aunt Paralee (I believe) or it could have been Aunt Lula came running to my rescue. Picture this, we are out in the country, no running water and the fire was raging. We used broken limbs from the pines and slapped the fire and we also used old clothes that we wetted down and finally got it under control before it reach the timberline. Needless to say, I couldn't sit down for a few days after the whipping I got. I didn't get any sympathy about my burnt hands and feet either. I learned a valuable lesson that day. Never and I repeat NEVER start a fire outdoors on a windy day. As I listen now to the news of forest fires out of control I can see how easily one starts. Careless campers or smokers are most often the culprits that are guilty of starting these and the damages that can be done over someone not taking the time to think before they act.

I suppose that is enough of my past that will give you a sense of where I came from and where I was going and how I got to be the person that you know and, I hope, love. After being married for 22 years off  and on and raising my two wonderful children, I moved on to another marriage with the Sunshine of my life. It has been 30 years so far and I'm looking forward to many more years with Clyde Gentry, my sunshine.

He gave me my wings to fly, to go to school so that I could get a job that ended at the Booth Western Art Museum in Cartersville, GA. I am employed as the research librarian and had to self-teach myself how to be a librarian. I had never heard of Library of Congress Classification so I fell back upon the words I received from my grandmother and gave it a try and learned all I could.

Now they call me their "Looney Librarian" because if I can't have fun doing my job I'll stay home in bed. I never get up not wanting to come to work. I love my job. When you love your job, it isn't work, it's a blessing.

Use these next blank pages to write down your own memories.

_____

_____

_____

_____

_____

_____

_____

_____

_____

_____

_____

_____

_____

_____

_____

_____

_____

_____

_____

_____

_____

Memories

_____

_____

_____

_____

_____

_____

_____

_____

_____

_____

_____

_____

_____

_____

_____

_____

_____

_____

_____

_____

_____

_____

Memories

_____

_____

_____

_____

_____

_____

_____

_____

_____

_____

_____

_____

_____

_____

_____

_____

_____

_____

_____

_____

_____

_____

Memories

Thank You

for reading our books!

Look for other books

Published by

www.TMPbooks.com